MW01593385

NATIVE MOONS, NATIVE DAYS

Text Copyright © 2012 Carol Willette Bachofner
Native New England Authors Series Volume 7

Published by Bowman Books
P.O. Box 308,
Greenfield Center, New York 12833
nativeauthors.com
518-584-1728

ISBN 978-1-105-25454-3

Printed in the United States of America

NATIVE MOONS, NATIVE DAYS

poems by Carol Willette Bachofner

Table of Contents

Prologue

In the Abenaki tradition, as for many Native tribes, there were once 13 months, corresponding to the 28 day cycles of the full moon. These months now encompass a longer cycle. Only February remains as 28 days. However, in nature, the original cycle remains. The moon's fullness remembers the old way. This cycle of moons makes sense in practical terms. For example, winter is the "folding in" time when most of the work of the tribes was completed. Crops were harvested, hides had been prepared. Families had often moved to "winter camp" in order to shelter together during the inclement weather certain to come. Unlike summertime when there was a glut of physical labor, this was a time for being together, sharing, learning, surviving.

It is in the spirit of this cycle that the following poems are offered. The poems are small stories, teaching and extending a look into the way the modern Abenaki (Alnôbak, Aln8bak) sees the world in light of the history and/or language of the People, with a sense of new stories to be told. Woven in with these fragments of story are the moons themselves. These appear chronologically, where the stories do not necessarily. At the end of the collection are two epilogues, the final one an imaginative, missing, thirteenth moon.

A glossary of Abenaki words is offered at the end of the poems, to lend meaning to the unfamiliar, consonant-laden words of the language. It is important for the reader to be able to see these words as they are in the old language. A visitor may notice that New England, Ndakinna, is full of strange-looking place names, and wonder where they originate. These are words from the original language of the place, like Piscataqua or Agamenticus (river & mountain names), and whole towns such as Norridgewock or Sebago. Over time, some place names have been altered in terms of spelling, or in pronunciation, but they remain in some form. For tribal people of the northeast, coming upon a place name in some version of the old language is like finding a long-lost relative in the pages of the phone book of a visited town.

Origin

Everything started over water:
bows, arrows, winds gathering, pulling
primal ocean into the air, sending
it back in swirls, funnels, swells. At first
nothing but water, and over water, air.
Blue air filled with people. Over water,
a hole in the clouds and a woman
looking through, dreaming and falling.

Abazenoda, An Abenaki Basket Tale

— this is the place my story camps

The Maker, *Dabaldak* walked
around the place he made,
Ndakinna. It overflowed
with good things. Streams tumbled
their banks with fresh water and fish. The woods
boomed with the rutting music of moose. Redwings
and chickadees kept the count.

But Dabaldak was joyless, needed
people to keep him
company, to love *Ndakinna*
and keep it well. So he raised his bow and shot
an arrow straight into the belly
of the brown ash, *Maahlakws.* It trembled
and heaved until the first two-leggeds came out,
carrying their lives in a beautiful basket,
woven from the bark of their mother.
　　　　　They came out, these Only People.

Evolution

Think of the feeling the sky has
when it begins to fall, changes itself
into a liquid, slips perfectly over deep mountains
and valleys, making a home for those without
feet or legs strong enough to be vertical.

Think of the sea
choppy and cold, hiding secrets
older than the land it covers
set forth when the waters parted
making the sky lose itself to gravity
no longer hovering over a formless mass
but shedding itself by droplets,
then changing its mind and pulling back.

Think of the archaeopteryx,
not bird or dragon, but bony winged freak
waiting to be a museum piece. Or of the man
down the street whose frame has bent so far
that it is nearly fossil, scapulae folding
and fragile, legs crouching like the ancient frog,
fingers clawed and brittle.

What a study
we will all make one day, with our jaws
wired open anatomically correct,
our vertebrae held in place and erect again,
no one guessing how much cowering
got us there. Or how much we yearned
to get back into the sea, or up into the blue sky.

Alnôbaiwi

We turn to the sea, feel the tide pulling,
see something coming. We turn our hands in the earth
to the corn growing greener day by day,
spending time with her sisters, ready to feed us.

In our way, Alnôbaiwi, it is best to sleep with the head
in the east, making it easy to see the coming sun.
In our way, we are always facing something,
seeing what others don't see coming.

Greetings Moon *Alamikos*

Hungry wolves cry back
and forth to mourn easy food. Hunting
hard for us too, everything edible buried.
Cemeteries are closed for winter,
no lowering of the dead
into the frozen earth, overhead
trailing stars, a road
where the ancestors gather
to greet their relatives.

Naming Water

Gwantigok, Penobscot,
    Passamaquoddy, Pashipakokee,
long rivers, long through the land you flow
long through us will you flow,
flowing from where the rocks widen,
from where pollack feed us.

Piscataqua, Androscoggin, Cobbosseecontee,
    Olamantegok, Quahog,
where water lies between the hills
through the sheltering place,
to where sturgeon gather together
to red ochre river, color of our children.
Shellfish place, treaty-making place.

Sebastivcook, Seninebik,
    Skowhegan, Baskahegan,
our stories flow
through little channels,
bearing rocks and memories
from where salmon leap the falls
to broad open waters,

turning back to where wild onions grow,
With birch and ash along their backs,
long rivers of first light
through our families flowing:
Wazwtegok, Winoztegok,
    Zawakwtegw, Gwantigok.

    Ndakinna.

Anthropologies

Plant a rose
by your kitchen door
and disturbing news

of past civilizations
rises up like sap
into the leaves.

The scent of their blood
translates itself
into fragrant red petals.

You can't dig
down a single inch
without raising the dead.

Winter Bringer

Winter Bringer:
my name in tribal language, the moon bringing
winter, bringing me. Ice hangs outside
the delivery room windows, *pkwamiak,*
like teeth from an old smile, like drips of cream
down the sides of the bowl where gingerbread
soaks up five-hundred-year old snow.

Anhaldamawigizos

It's New Year's Day
and the snow from last year,
from yesterday's icy rain,
is pock-marked and dusky. The weather
report is bright with promises
of clean white dust. Dare I hope
for heaps of forgiveness only the sky
offers, for snow angels on the lawn?
Black ice and black moods be gone!
Throw out the Christmas casserole
at the back of the fridge.

I try to forgive, as is our way,
but I hold on to your harsh remark,
your wagged finger.
I want to let go
of your sleeping too early, leaving
me alone
in front of the tv.

I ought to ask you to forgive me, too.
I should say the words
prescribed by my ancestors:
anhaldam mawi kassipalilawalan

I could go to bed with you,
do what you love,
what I promised.
But I'm afraid to talk
about vows snapped like eaves ice.

So I've sewn my lips shut
like the dragonfly does to those who lie,
bright green needle body flickering,
wings brushing against my cheek.

Wazôliinebi

In our way, snow is water
that feeds us without walking to the stream.
Our way, *beboniwi*, the winter way,
snow lets us rest from the work we do,
from pulling corn and tomatoes
and canning squash that grew like hair
nourished by *wazôliinebi*
while we watched over them.
We turn in bed and listen to snow
whispering about corn.

Skin Talk

If I sold my skin
to an art dealer
it would get tooled,
stretched, decorated
until I no longer
feel the pain of giving in.
You paint me
as stubborn. But see!
I am flexible. I give
with the tugs and pulls,
mold myself to fit,
to agree, to get along.

But my skin is not for sale,
trade, or stealing.
I paint myself with earth,
russet & ochre.
I go outside singing
to Grandmother Moon,
who calls me perfect, beautiful.

Wazônliskik

There's a little snow on the ground
and more on the way. I welcome it
and bring some inside to boil for tea.
I watch birds use it for bathing, fluffing
themselves without a single thought of freezing.
There's a little snow today and tomorrow
and then it will be spring. That's how it works.
So many people try to get away from snow
that there are fewer and fewer footprints
in it, fewer and fewer pots of snow tea.

Bough Shedding Moon *Bigôdagos*

Branches rattle their cast-offs
against the windows, *Pkwamiak,*
like knives grazing the panes as they go.
It is a darker time than other moons,
eclipsed by earth's own shadow,
snowed in and hungry. The jaw opens
and nothing fills it, the mouth moves
to sing, but the notes freeze
in rooms we don't heat. The kettle
wants snow for tea, and you cover me
while you slip outside for some.
I will make you warm again, will open
my mouth for your tongue, wet and cold
from tasting the powder outside our door.

Cegwalôwzia

You ask of my health and I say it, the joking thing
cegwalôwzia. I feel like a frog. Now you,
you might say there is one in your throat, messing up
that perfect speaking voice, the song for church.
I say it to mean I could croak from this flu.

Defined by Water, *Nebiwi*

In the *Pashipakokee,* river spirits call
out our names, names that live
under our skins. Can't you feel it
when the water comes by, moving
your blood a little faster, bubbling
over your muscles? You are alive in it,
defined by water old as the sky
that keeps its portrait. Science tells us
we are 70% water, but that's a lie.
We are all water, the water of home.
The river listens to our stories and remembers
for the time when our voices will fail.
We call to the stones and they roll down
stream to our children, tell them
that we are drying out, becoming *nesowadnehunk.*

Sleep Out

away from tight walls
heater blasting all night,
tick-tocking clock in the hall,
creaking bathroom floor,
dripping shower head.

Sleep out where stars burn
steady, waves' pendula swing,
fanning the scent of sea .
It's a cool pillow of sand
that needs no turning.

See like a night animal.
Ignore the scratch of twigs
against your back, the bite
of the mosquito, the river of sweat
between your shoulder blades.

Shed the shell grown over old stories,
negônôjemowôganal, over songs
in the old tribal language
passed along like river water.
Oligawi, sleep well, and they will wake in you.

Listen to your breathing as the sun comes
walking along the ground, jumping
like a frog from ripple to ripple over stones
in the river. Listen to the sea stretching,
sighing just beyond the trees.

Zôkhôban

After darkness is done
with the land, with dreamers,
and the half face, *babasôpkwao,* is gone
from the sky, light comes,
work begins again, all stories
jump up and reenact themselves
around the table. Where is that firefly
that went too close to the lamp?
What happened to the frog
that twittered in last night's bog?
Gizanda, Monday. Full of sparks.

Pond Water

It gets up your nose
when you roll the kayak,
gets in your blood after summers at the pond.
It will always call to you,
will always know when you return.
Maybe there's a splinter from the dock, still
deep in your heel, a small sliver
that seemed healed over. Maybe once a year
the spot reddens, pinches a little, a signal
to pack your shorts and bathing suit,
get in your car and head back
where, even in midsummer, it gets dark
early, save for the light the pond makes.

Moose Hunting Moon *Mozokas*

There must be fog in the woods I think,
so loud the sound, a moaning at sunrise,
but I remember it is moose hunting moon
and this is a warning. We tell each other
there's no use going to the thicket
where we had that June picnic, not now
when it's impossible to dodge the inevitable
arrow that makes only a little sizzle,
until it splits ribcage, breastbone, heart.
We tell each other that the moose
know where to hide, unless one of the hunters
prays for him to make the sacrifice. Fogged
in around us, the sounds of lovers calling
to take the baby and go deeper, *godlaka.*

The Old Man's Walk

Franconia, NH May 2003

They (white men) say (declare officiously)
that sometime in the night (which night they do not know)
in the deep fog of the White Mountains,
The Old Man fell to his death
crumbling into Profile Lake.

In truth (so say the Abenaki, his relatives)
he has been struggling to go home
to his wife for years now. Under the watchful
protection of the fog people, he broke free
of the bolts and cables
that held him for decades.
Wlipamkaani, travel well,
Old Man, Grandfather of the Granite,
long-suffering husband, watchful ancestor.

There is a lot of falling being done these days,
but this old face did not fall. He took his long walk,
the walk we all take, alone, without fanfare
or time of death called by an attending physician.

I think he smiled, though he hadn't smiled
for a thousand years.
I think he smiled and called out *matosao,* enough,
trembled with longing for his wife and children,
and simply dove off the face of the mountain
into the mirror of time, into his own profile.

It is good sign that the Old Man decided to walk
the land again, free of the white man's cords of steel.
Ohn, hohn, Grandfather, *wligonebi ...*
the water feels good against your brow.

Mamillômsen

The wind off the water
comes today with a new story,
Gedowbago, a noise in the water,
blown up like white caps and rollers.
The story brings names. French
English, any names that are foreign
must have surprised my relatives,
who spoke in consonants,
with vocables, vowels for music.
We decide to keep a few of the new names
in trade for them not killing us right away.

We Speak the White Man's Language

except when dreaming, except when our fingers
braid hair, weave blankets, knot bait bags,
when we are praying in Indian. Work brings words
from the belly, the soles of the feet.
Words walk the woods where our relatives
burned the way forward from camp to camp,
trading stories with people along the way.
We speak in our own tongues, syllables full
of consonants, echoing from the back
of the throat to the nose, to the wind.
Our words are a clearing, a place for fire.
Where did the language go when the black robes
threw holy water on it? Did it disappear
when the switch was on our backs? Into the trees,
into the streams, into our wombs to wait.

Alokada

Let's continue the work we laid down
while we slept and dreamed.
The all night walker, *Pôgwas*,
scrubbed the mountains
with borax while ghost fire flew
from the holes we'd dug
for the dead. It could power
a thousand cars across the desert,
run 3.5 million iPods for a day.
Tuesday, *Nizda alokan*. Filled with spirits.

Sugar Making Moon *Zogalikas*

Steam rises from the baffles,
pure maple, bubbling over, then settled
by a dollop of pure butter, sweetening itself
as it boils down and down. Dark
amber, medium or light, the drawn off
syrup a maine-stay for the oncoming
tourist season. But today is Maple Sunday
and the whole of it is for us who stay.
No taste better than cold vanilla ice cream
drizzled with this morning's batch
and eaten on the porch. *Gluskabi* told
us we'd have to work harder
to get *zogalinebi*, the syrup that once dripped ready
from the branches. We were a lazy people
willing to lie down and be fed by the trees.
Now we tap and boil and evaporate,
work from daylight to dark, feeding everyone.

Zogalinebi

It runs thin and over my hands. Not sweet now,
not syrupy enough for pancakes.
I lick my palms, give thanks.
Boiling time, and the steam rises
to the mountains like a stream going backwards.
I can see the clouds over Katahdin
as they grow fat and sweet from drinking it.
It will rain later over land
that is always giving something back.
Most people will never know
that what waters their perfect gardens
is a gift from the maples
they grumble about, want to cut down.

Blood Snow

Think of blood in a leaf,
how it feeds the stalk
until it dries like tears
and every blossom drops,

of sugar in the maple,
how it runs like blood
from the wound in its side,
and everyone is fed.

Think of blood in the wrist,
how it is sent there
chamber by chamber,
with every beat counted,

of the leaves of the heart,
opening and closing,
running against death,
until it lies down in the snow.

There are rivers

flowing by in the night, returning to the sea,
and they remember me, know my name.
There are fish schooled in the stories
of my people, singing the old language,
songs they keep for us. There are stones, smoothed
in battle, rounded by footfall, stones
that consider me a relative, say my name.
I will not drown here in the swift current or slow pools.
I will not die with a sharp suck of mud in my lungs
as the land moves like liquid in spring. No river
will take me until I am ripe, like the acorn
or the ash bark. Then these rivers,
rivers of *Ndakinna* will willingly give me up
to the sea, the most ancient water, the elder sister.

Long May It Run

this Kootenai, silver green
ribbon around the Cabinet Mountains,
this fishing ground where midges and flies
hop the surface in an ancient dance,
the same dance the two-leggeds did,
they who fished in the old way,
with poplar poles and weirs, spinning
their lines out across the water
and making offerings of tobacco.

The fish gave themselves as food
and families were filled.
Only take the old males was the call.
The two-leggeds knew the circle,
spared the women and their roe.

Long may the water flow
over the sunlit passage, across
cold depths where rainbows and browns
wait for the flick of the line overhead,
signal that the circle is still moving,
their time is now.

What young man carved his first flute here,
sang his courting song? What woman knelt
and scooped out the day's water?
This tribal river knows its own history.
Listen to the larks in the bitterroot
sing it; hear the waters repeat the refrain.
Over and over the stones it drums,
celebrating, warning, passing
every ancient story along.

Sign Language

Lift up your feathered eyes
and watch the red-tailed hawk rise
to a black hinge, opening wide,
closing. His silent fan of wing
breaks the code that unlocks the sky.
He knows how. He knows why.

River of Fields

Kikôtegw, cultivation of a people
by the French, a new way of farming
that seems efficient. But corn
is confused without her sisters, won't toss
her yellow hair, *skamoniodebkwanal* in happiness
now that she has to stand alone on the bank
of this river of fields. Squash wanders all over,
looking for support. Beans snap on the vine,
lose focus. *Alnôbaiwi*, the sisters stood all day
huddled up and sharing what they knew.
Rivers should stay rivers, and fields
should be wide and unending until
they reach the ash and birch or the sea.

Zobagw

We paddle beyond the jetty
into open water where traps are lowered
and raised, morning and afternoon ---
haul, haul, haul away ---
filled with lobsters, *zôgak*, for people
who come to the docks for food.
The magic bird, *medawihla,*
is off the sea now, dressed in black
and white checks, bringing her babies on her back.
Hear her on the ponds now, clear as morning.
Wednesday, *Nseda alokan.* Full bellies.

Harvesting at the Stream

Fiddleheads push
to the edge of the water,
and wait for instruction
from the elders,
wait for us to bend
for them.
The curve of their backs is fetal.
Heads tucked in reverence, they speak
softly to those who need feeding.
Take me, I offer myself.

Abenaki Bones

*a reflection on the failure
of King Philip's War*

Our bones fled north,
paddled icy waters, carried
stories and songs to Odanak
across the Ouelle River.

Bones ran from Pennacook,
from Norridgewock and Ossipee,
from Saco and Kennebec,
bones running through the night.

Our bones scattered
in bloody fields,
in sad forests,
far from winter camp.

The enemy believed
our bones ruined,
cut down like corn,
burned to meal and ash.

But Abenaki bones are strong,
leaning together
around old stories, in new camps.

Planting Moon *Kikas*

Plunging hands into warm earth
where worms have shed casts, have moved
and gone through every seed row,
we take care to plant
the way our ancestors taught, sisters
together for strength and company.
We lean on each other too, family stories wound
around and strong in the northeast wind that
blows off the sea, that tries our memory.
She is *wasawak,* squash.
You are *adebakwal*, beans. *Kakiknia,* I am corn.

Jijiz

They might be endangered,
can hardly be found
except by the Abenaki
who know where to look,
as they knew where
they had hung their cradle boards.
But there it was, on the sale table
at the botanical gardens, *jijiz*,
a Jack-in-the-pulpit, alone
and not feeling safe at all
from the docents who commented
that this was a rare one indeed
and wouldn't it look grand
in your rock garden. I paid six dollars
to free this one, to hide him
behind the lilacs in my yard
where the proper ladies
of the Botanical Society never go.

Bitten

it's true
you could
bleed out
bitten
over two
hours by
nine thousand
mosquitos

science
tells us
these truths
and we
believe

or not

until
at night
we hear
the buzz.

Hoeing Moon *Nokkahigas*

Strike rocks from the rows
of corn, beans and squash. Stoop
together around the stalks, *alnôbaiiwi.*
Pull straggler weeds, make clear the way.
It is how we care for our sins,
rooting them out, bending our backs
over them with steel edged hoe and shovel,
pouring fire on the pile of them, blotting
an easy rise. Every vine needs the hoe
to open the ground for water, for growing
higher and stronger than untended food.
Every blossoming comes after the pain
of the precise cut, and finally water storm
clouds held, then released upon the garden.

Aiyamihaw8gan

Pray for a change in the weather,
for a blue cloud, white sky day,
a day of possibility:
songbirds speaking
the old language, *Aln8bak*
in the trees,
snails out of their shells
and dancing.

Let's have a sluice
through puddles,
get our new shoes wet, run naked
in the kaleidoscope
of a sudden shower.

The kind of day we need is
an upside
downside, in-the-middle-of-the-lake day
with no oars in the canoe,
a no life jacket, a day
feeling loon song on our breasts
and hearing stories
they tell us as they dive deep into memory.

Let's pray that tonight
will bring the old ones from where
they have been waiting, from the river
where they have been singing.

Bring your pipe, your flute, your firstborn
and come with the next perfect story.

Blueberry Making Moon *Zataikas*

Bucks in new antlers, hay
in barns, thunderstorms
ranging the mountains, wetting
the seashore. In the barrens, fruit
bursts blossoms open, grey-blue
crowned berries, super food
they say now. *Alnôbakiak*, we knew
for thousands of years, thick
custard of pale blue sustaining
us before the first snows.

Cowissewachook

Rough mountain, windfall mountain
what can you see from there?
Can you see me here in the meadow,
worrying in the afternoon heat?
Can you see where the eagle nests,
pair of eggs delicate and vulnerable
ready to split -- and *kaamoji!*
the line continues, flying off the lists
we made to save them? Rough mountain
windfall mountain, what will I find there
where you cover the sky?
Yawda alokan, Thursday. Full of questions.

Harvesting Moon Demezôwas

Walk out under the moon that fills
the whole sky just as it rises. Walk bare
foot to the trees that sing their evening song.
Wajemi, kiss me, promise we
will have a good harvest. Lie down with me
in the rows of squash and pumpkins, fecund
bellies ready to burst their vines. Feel the heartbeat
of your mother, thrum and ache of every pulse.
Alosada, Gezaldami, out into the garden
to see what the maker has left for us.

Mijowôgankas

It is the eating month. August or September,
when harvest comes in and there's so much
squash, beans, corn that we spend every day
eating it, canning it, drying it. Famine is only truth
because the lie they've been telling people is that food
only grows in bins at the grocery store, or comes
from California, where watering is run-off
from the detritus left by animals
trapped in pens and fed hormones to grow fat,
passing on poison the Maker never intended for us.
But in our gardens the three sisters flourish,
wrapped in each other's arms and singing
harvest songs taught long ago by the grandmothers.

Corn Making Moon   Skamonkas

Silk on stalks soughing
in the strong wind that comes
to scatter seed, take down the heat.
Alokada, nidôba, come to the fields
and gather in what we need. *Micida*,
let's feast on what is offered. The sisters
are ready to rest again in their mother's lap.
Children burst from the follicles
of play, taller and stronger, hair
blowing behind like flags of summer.

Rituals With Fish

Step into the river, wade out
where your ancestors have stood
for thousands of years.

Bait, cast, retrieve, release.
Weather read, canoe balance,
reel, reel, reel.

Catch, gut, eat.
Steelhead, rainbow, hornpout,
muskie, perch.

They fin close, dare, dart.
It's a dance we do, that feeds us,
that keeps us in the water
that gave us to the earth.

A Sister Flies Ahead of Me Now

for EK (Kim) Caldwell 1954-1997

I discover you
not unlike the way Columbus supposed
he had discovered us;
you were already there ... settled,
imposing, beautiful, shining in the light of morning.

We sit, reeking of sage, flying to gather
in the Oneida woods. In the old way
of asking, we find each other sisters in the family
circle of word weavers, of story singers, water bearers.

Your smiles collect on my shoulders and my ears
ring with your words. We are women, satisfied
to sit with our saged-up bodies
and learn of each other. We have husbands,
write poems to stay alive, love being brown.
I know you a thousand days by the end
of our five hour flight.

Now you fly overhead. I cup my eyes, shadow
the sun to see you. Yesterday I caught a breath
of sage in the grocery store, thought you might be there
buying oranges or bread for dinner. I walk past
the waft of memory, hear you chuckle.
I buy the oranges myself, crying and laughing.

My sage is safe in the eagle bag you gave me
when we met. You are there too in the twist
of red cloth, in the pocket of my coat
where my hand touches your gift. I send you sparks
of fire, prayers to where you fly. You are
a brown, round, woman of the air, circling me
and giving me new songs to sing, new words
to weave. How do I begin to miss you.

Leaf Falling Moon *Benibagos*

Bobatama, pray for one another
as leaves fall and we see darkness
coming for us, downstream and in the forest
streams where weirs are tightened, where hunters snap
their bows and load their rifles for the hunt.
Zoziwaldam, be lonely, for the birds
that have flown off the branches, for lobsters
that dive and hide in colder water. *Nonogaiwi,*
soon enough, it will be winter and we will rest
in our blankets, feet to the warm stove
where hunters' stew bubbles and steams.
Mekwabi, Pray for fire to keep away the darkness.

Jibaaki

I want to enter the ground slowly,
sift down in ashy snow to the beach
when the sea is out.
I want you to burn me there
and watch the sun coming up
to get my spirit across the water
and into the sky, a process
not like *Bostoniwi* death rituals
with pink formalin replacing blood,
stitched up neck and wrist hidden
under the best outfit in the closet.

I want to be dressed
in the clothes I made, decorated
with shells I found, fringed around
the edges, like the sky in a storm.
Wrap me tight in my turtle blanket
so my arm won't suddenly jut out
scaring the partygoers. It's okay
to steam the lobster if you dig
a hole deep enough to meet
federal standards for public safety.
I think there might be rules
about burning an Indian woman
on the beach, even at low tide.

Burial Dress

Carefully   Prayerfully

Inside, outside   Sinew sewn

Our Ways   of   Old Days

Ash and Fire   Spirit home

Elk skin   Doe skin

Supple, softened   Forest grown

Breath dress   in   Death dress

Shell and Bead   Woman's own

Fingering   Fringing

Back, forth   Together alone

Gentle sway   of   Whitened frays

Platform and Pyre   Indian bones

Unknown Algonquin Females, Circa 1800s

They dug up my grandmother, moved her
to the museum. No one stopped them.
I had no say. De-recognized by government,
filed at the BIA under "I" (*Indian, former*),
she's been reduced to anthropology, curated
by bureaucrats, her bones on display
with the bones of a woman from an enemy tribe:
(*Unknown Algonquin Females, Circa 1800s*)
No one sang a travel song for her to ease her bones
along the way; no giveaway, no mourning strings
to soften the sorrow. I have watched their grandmas
prayed and cried into the ground, names cut
into marble, bodies preserved under stones safe
behind iron gates. The governor's announcement claims
today: *There are no Abenaki Indians left in Vermont.*

Catch and Release

Reeling, snapping, hooking, so much to do
so much for the one
moment when the shine breaks the surface,
flesh-heavy. Breakfast at Mt. Blue campground
when it was still okay to eat the perch
we caught. But no more eating, no more
sounds of frying coming to me
in the tent, 12 x 12 and reeking of water
repellent. Catch, release, find something to eat
grown in dirt. The perch must wonder
why we reject their sacrifice.
Skawatekwigizegad. Friday. Filled with regret.

Bow Echo

A bow echo came
to the sky
sharp fork bent
the afternoon
'til it snapped, green
and yellow arcs
flinched over the house
and trees hanged themselves
by the chords.

Ice Forming Moon *Mezatanos*

Set traps, *onegigwibona* before the ice
comes down from the mountains, spreads
its hands and shakes the land, cracks
rivers' backs, breaks our steps.
Beavers slap and dive, hides
thickening, coats a lure for hunters.
It is a great dance, ice
billowing up from the bottom of the river
beavers pushing down through the crust
to safety, *naaiaiak* waiting to open the traps.

At the Edge of Something

Low haze overhanging
the meadow makes snow
darken, sign of warmer weather coming.
At the edge of every drift a few
wishes scattered at equinox begin
coming true. Soon enough sounds
of new birds singing
and the whole place will soften,
become a medicine field, *nebizokikônek,*
and flowers will mouth the rain.
But first, there is the pushing
the breaking of the caul.
Gadawsanda. Wanting to be Sunday,
Saturday. Full of longing.

Abenaki Divorce

Get out!
Go back!
To your mother!

I leave a bundle
(his belongings, nothing else)
by the door.

Without fanfare,
I remit him back
    to where he started.

If it were only that simple, that final.

16 years and I am finally rid of
the last piece of him:
a watch (not working) belonging to his uncle.
It was time.

I still see his name
on the check he writes
every month.
I'd prefer
a credit card payment,
direct deposit.

To rid yourself of a cantankerous man
and all of his detritus:

> *lay a line of blessed tobacco*
> *along the doors and windows;*
> *smudge yourself with sage and cedar;*
> *dance with your hair down*
> *at the moon's waning.*

Equidia/equinox

In one breathless shudder
within the hiding away time,
the earth rolls quietly to a stop.
So finite and rare is the moment,
it is dared only at the exact halves
of each year, and goes mostly unnoticed.

Norridgewock Religion

20 paces from the east gate, 60 feet long by 25.
40 Abenaki boys in cassocks, playing Catholic games
and looking for a way out. A large handsome building
burned in 1705, built again on the backs of the Abenaki
who converted to stay alive. Johnson Harmon wrote his friend
that this was a monument to progress, this log
church adorned with pictures and toys to please the natives.
Fr. Rasles, black robes and white bread,
shot through and through defending the people, this church.
The bell was cut down and buried in the woods.
Abenaki blood flowed like communion wine into the Kennebec.

Land Sickness

I'm flung away, flung far from the edges
of ocean, beneath brown, unsettled skies;
I have no salt spray for my hair, no chill
gray sand beneath my feet. I am bereft
of crisp ocean kisses and wild seaweed,
dancing like a sultry lover around my ankles.
Perhaps I will die from land sickness, this
never-ending orphanage from Maine's shore.
Soon they will find my body, petrified and blue
in a corner of the desert, eyes squeezed shut
against fetid breeze and fiery desert sky.
In one tight fist will they find a single drop
of salt, a tear that began in the surf at home.

A Trade, Like the Old Ways

Because I put up with sand
that had long forgotten water,
that had been chewed by a rabid sun,
that had all but given up on green,
I need to go home.

I need to thrust my feet
between cold wet grains, take up space
with hermit crabs and urchins, spread
my toes in tidal pools alive with ancestors' lives
I need to respect.

Because I remember deep in my muscles
what they felt as they moved to the sea
for summering, because I feel what they felt
as salt etched their faces, because I am
part of every ebb and neap of sea,
I need to make an offering.

I propose a trade, a something
of myself in exchange for what I might carry:
a cutting of 40 pieces of flesh
was once the barter. But I am squeamish
after long exile in a whitened life.
I offer only smoke, in my grandmother's pipe.

Sealed by salt and smoke,
the trade is complete: a small glass bottle
of sand swinging from my neck
in a dance my people would do: a sway and thump,
counterclockwise, a beat not so different
from what moves in my veins.

History

is always happening:

like last week
when

lit by a wooden match,
a thousand acres
of old trees burned.

Or yesterday
when

people began hoarding
water in glass jars, like the ones
grandmothers used to
conserve
peaches and rhubarb.

Around your neck,
history too

in the soft pouch where
your umbilical cord
remains as evidence

that you once got along
perfectly
with your mother.

Loops of collapsed
vein and arteries testify,
flattened hard like amber:

your dna suspended
like a hind leg or a bee's wing.

Zogwawon

I paint my face, double curves
on each cheek and across the brow.
I choose the colors of war, red and black,
kelegatsta, each stripe a memory of some wrong.
I want yellow for the dawn, for peace.
Bring trickster clowns to shake the rattles,
no more *baskhodebahiganal* to break the heads
of our enemies. No more shouts of insult.

Winter Bringing Moon *Bebonkas*

Full cold moon, white eye long
over the horizon, small heat over a cold sea,
moon before yule, gift of the maker
to lead us to winter camp, burn slow
and steady to keep company
with the ancestors. Long night moon,
bring stories, gleaming tooth
in the dark mouth, *agamokawi*, teach me. Bring
fire that will not burn away as we sleep,
facing east, facing what is coming.

Wlôwatawak

Blue tea, strong aroma of woods and orchids
in the fine china cup left me
by my grandmother. She always left things
at the edge of the woods, bits of
wool for birds, first plates of every meal
for the little people who care for us
while we sleep. She made a habit
of leaving things in town too, mittens
and hats in the bins at Goodwill, shoes
on street corners where bums
could just walk into them. Books
she left whenever she went to the bank,
making a deposit, she said, *for the future.*
But for me, she left tribal stories
told over cups of blue tea,
and then this cup, her lips pressed
onto the rim so that even now, forty years
gone, I feel her kissing me, calling me her protégé.

On the Seventh Day

What is the language of this place?
In summer it is everything, everywhere,
all at once beautiful, dangerous, dying.
The sun grows hotter, forcing us to weep
over every cell that burns.
In the woods, *skwedaibbagok*, fire leaf, comes
after flame, resurrection.
A small stick becomes tree, you & I become
because of trees. Deep furrows hold
secrets, waiting to spring
up and become forest again, now that Sun
has finished his burning. He is field-maker,
forest maker, shouting in whispers before he sleeps:
Sanda, Sanda, Sanda. Sunday. Full of rest.

Epilogue

Baskaba, Open Water

We move to the shore, toward open water,
all things winter done, fires sanded and cold.
Time to say goodbye to cousins, uncles, and aunties,
to kiss the cheeks of grandparents and wish
them good travel, *Wlipamkaani*. All has been said
around the fire, all is ready for the long days.
Families walk or paddle to the shore,
looking east where everything is new.
Maanamagwas, the osprey, circles overhead
and welcomes us. Days lengthen toward the horizon.
We look to the sky to see who is falling, who is rising.

Epilogue 2

What Old Moon?

In the new way, on the new calendar,
twelve moons, like apostles, gather
around the sun which defines
the days. What old moon has gone
from the sky to make room
for the things we rush to? Appointments
meeting this or that requirement, checks
deposited, markets shopped
for plastic food with ingredients
no one can pronounce. What moon went
missing in the dark of a new moon,
during a night so black no one noticed
it had been sent away. Or does it live
behind the sun, where the ancestors dance
in its ivory light, where the maker
praises its beautiful face? What name
has disappeared from the winter count?

Glossary

Glossary of Abenaki Terms
(in the order in which they appear in the poems)

Abazenoda ... basket made in the traditional manner
Ndakinna ... the land, Place of Dawn, Dawnland
Maahlakws .... brown ash, sacred creation tree of the Abenaki
Alnôbaiwi ... in the Abenaki way or manner
Bostoniwi ... in the American way or manner
Alamikos ... Greetings Moon
pkwamiak ... icicles
anhaldam mawi kassipalilawalan ... forgive me if I have wronged you, a traditonal utterance in the Forgiveness Month of January (*Anhaldamawigizos*)
wazôliinebi ... snow water, melting snow
wazônliskik ... a little snow on the ground
Bigôdagos ... Bough Shedding Moon
Cegwalôwzia ... a joking reply to inquiries about health, literally "I feel like a frog"
Nebiwi ... in water, what is in water
Pashipakokee ... Sheepscot River
nesowadnehunk ... dead water
negônôjemowôganal ... old stories
oligawi ... sleep well
zôkhôban ... ocean or sea
zôgak ... lobsters
medawihla ... loon
Nseda alokan ... Wednesday
babasôpkwao ... half moon
Gizanda ... Monday
godlaka   go hide
Mozokas ... Moose Hunting Moon
wlipamkaani ... travel well, a traditional farewell
matosao ... it is ended
ohn, hohn ... yes indeed
wligonebi ... the water feels good
Mamillômsen ... the wind that blows off the water or comes ashore
Alokada ... Let's work
Pôgwas ... moon, literally one who walks all night
Nizda alokan... Tuesday
Gedowbago ... it is a noise in the water

Zogalikas Sugar Making Moon
Gluskabi ... the maker, owner, man who made himself out of nothing
Zogalinebi, sap water, from the maple
Gluskabi ... storyteller, trickster, teacher of lessons
Katahdin ... sacred mountain of the Abenakis
Kikôtegw ... river of fields, literally a different way of farming proposed by the French settlement
at Norridgewock
kamoniodebkwanal ... corn silk, corn hair
Kikas Planting Moon
wasawak place of squash
adebakwal place of beans growing
Kakiknia I am corn
Nokkahigas Hoeing Moon
Jijiz ... "Jack-in-the-pulpit," plant that resembles a baby in a cradle board
aiyamihaw8gan ... prayer
Aln8bak ... the traditional name of the Abenaki people; the 8 is a vocable sounding like "ohn"
and is sometimes spelled "ô"
Alnôbakiak Abenaki culture
Cowissewachook ... Mt. Kearsarge in NH

kaamoji! ... oh wow! for crying out loud!

Yawda alokan ... Thursday

Zataikas Blueberry Making Moon

Demezôwas Harvesting Moon

Wajemi kiss me
Alosada, Gezaldami Walk with me, darling
Mijowôgankas ... the eating month, either August or September
Skamonkas Corn Making Moon
Alokada, nidôba Let's work, friend
Micida Let's eat
Benibagos ... Leaf Falling Moon

Bobatama, pray for one another

Zoziwaldam, be lonely, for the birds

*Nonogaiwi,*soon enough.

Mekwabi, Pray

Jibaaki ... funeral practice of scaffold burial, literally a forest of coffins

Bostoniwi ... in the American way or manner

Skawatekwigizegad ... Friday

Mezatanos Ice Forming Moon

onegigwibona set traps

naaiaiak people from downstream, people from away

nebizokikônek ... garden
Gadawsanda ... Saturday, wants to be Sunday

skwedaibbagok ... fire leaf, that which grows after being burned
zogwawon ... face paint
kelegatsta ... painted stripes
baskhodebahiganal ... war club or weapon (literally a head-breaker)
Wlôwatawak ... blue tea, between green & black
Bebonkas Winter Bringing Moon
agamokawi teach me
Sanda ... Sunday, day of recreation or rest
Baskaba ... open water
Maanamagwas ... osprey

Acknowledgments

The author would like to thank the editors of the following journals in which some of these poems appeared previously:

Land Sickness: My Home As I Remember

Origin: *The Cream City Review*, Vol 27.1

A Sister Flies Ahead of Me Now : Gatherings, Vol. IX

Blood Snow: *The Comstock Review*

Burial Dress: Gatherings, Vol.XI

The Old Man's Walk: 2008 Poets' Guide to New Hampshire

About the Author

Carol Willette Bachofner, Abenaki, writes poems that show we are all connected, to each other and to nature. As an indigenous woman, she writes with a strong sense of place through narrative. Her poems have appeared in such notable journals as *Prairie Schooner, CT Review, Main Street Rag, The Comstock Review, Crab Orchard Review, The Cream City Review, Naugatuck River Review,* and others. Founding editor of Pulse Literary Journal, Carol teaches poetry in her community. Rockland, Maine and "on the road" via workshops and conferences. She was a featured speaker at the Maine Literary Festival in 2009, focusing her remarks on indigenous literature in the modern age. Bachofner has previously published three books of poetry: Daughter of the Ardennes Forest, Breakfast at the Brass Compass, and I Write in the Greenhouse. She founded the annual *Poetry Month Rockland,* a city-wide celebration of poetry. In 2011, Bachofner was a runner-up in the Maine Literary Awards, one of three finalists in the short works/poetry category. Visit her web site carolbachofner.com for links to her literary zine, her blog, and her facebook page.

The Native New England Authors Series

Made in the USA
Middletown, DE
28 July 2023

35850965R00050